The Lions' Gate

THE LIONS' GATE

Selected Poems of Titos Patrikios

Translated by Christopher Bakken
and Roula Konsolaki

Truman State University Press
New Odyssey Series

Published by Truman State University Press, Kirksville, Missouri
tsup.truman.edu
© 2006 Truman State University Press
New Odyssey Series
All rights reserved

Cover art: The Lions' Gate, Mycenae. © 2005 by Benaki Museum Athens.

Cover design: Teresa Wheeler
Type: Adobe Garamond, copyright Adobe Systems Incorporated
Printed by Thomson-Shore, Dexter, Michigan USA

Library of Congress Cataloging-in-Publication Data
Patrikios, Titos, 1928-
  [Poems. English. Selections]
  The lions' gate : selected poems of Titos Patrikios / translated by Christopher
    Bakken and Roula Konsolaki
    p. cm. — (New odyssey series)
  ISBN-13: 978-1-931112-64-2 (alk. paper)
  ISBN-10: 1-931112-64-9 (alk. paper)
  1. Patrikios, Titos, 1928—Translations into English. I. Bakken, Christopher,
    1967- II. Konsolaki, Roula. III. Title. IV. Series
  PA5627.A84A2 2006
  889.1'34—dc22
                                                                    2006033255

No part of this work may be reproduced or transmitted in any format by any means without written permission from the publisher.

The paper in this publication meets the minimum requirements of the American National Standard for Information Sciences—Permanence of Paper for Printed Library Materials, ANSI Z39.48-1992.

Truman State University Press is committed to preserving ancient forests and natural resources. We elected to print *The Lions' Gate* on 50% post consumer recycled paper, processed chlorine free. As a result, for this printing, we have saved:

4 Trees (40' tall and 6-8" diameter)
1,807 Gallons of Wastewater
727 Kilowatt Hours of Electricity
199 Pounds of Solid Waste
391 Pounds of Greenhouse Gases

Truman State University Press made this paper choice because our printer, Thomson-Shore, Inc., is a member of Green Press Initiative, a nonprofit program dedicated to supporting authors, publishers, and suppliers in their efforts to reduce their use of fiber obtained from endangered forests.

For more information, visit www.greenpressinitiative.org

Contents

Illustrations viii
Acknowledgments ix
Translators' Preface xi
Introduction xiii
The Lions' Gate 1

Early Poems (1948–1951)
    The Conquest of Everest 5
    Latest News 7
    The Friends 8
    Open Borders 9
    Fires 11
    Tavern "Abundance" 12

From *Exercises* (1952)
    Faces 15
    Paper 17

From *Dirt Road* (1952–1954)
    Earth and Sea 21
    Facing Up to the Sky 29

From *Years of the Stone* (1953–1954)
    Drafts on Makronissos 41
    Another Day in Ai-Stratis 44
    Frame for the Light 46
    Military March 47
    Monologue 48
    Verses, 1 49
    Habits of the Detainees 50
    Syllables 51
    Plaster Sky 52
    Night in the Tent 53

From *Litigations* (1955)
    While They Speak 57

    Carnival Night 58
    Last Light 59
    Tomorrow 60
    Three Dimensions 61
    Flesh 62

From *Apprenticeship* (1956–1959)
    Verses, 2 65

From *Apprenticeship Again* (1959–1962)
    To Learn 69
    My Hometown 70
    Elements of Identity 71
    Eight Years 74
    A Family Lunch 75
    The Door 76

From *Sea of Promise* (1959–1963)
    Cure 79
    The Blame 80
    Trip 81
    Letter 82
    Cold Wind 83
    Catacomb 84
    Encounter 85
    Double Moon 86
    Metro 87
    Via dei Coronari 123 88
    The Other Town 89
    Besieged Time 90
    Via di Tor Millina 91
    Villa Adriana 92
    The Message 93
    Gare du Nord 94

From *Deformities* (1959–1963)
    Persistence of a City 97

From *Optional Stop* (1967–1973)
    Secret Life 101
    Pretense 102

Demonstration 103
The Mountains. 104
Church of the Seven Sleepers 105
The Stone. 106
Foreign Skies 107
Waiting Area. 108
Woman 109
The Journey 111
Oedipus's Story. 112
Easter 113
Millennia 114
Allegory 115

From *Opposing Mirrors* (1988)
Verses, 3 119
A Town in Southern Greece 120
Zebras 121

From *The Pleasures of Extension* (1992)
My Language 125
Loves 126
Appropriation of Statues. 127

From *Resistance of the Facts* (2000)
Ashes 131
Nightmare 132
Molyvos, 1 133
Molyvos, 2 134
The Young Researcher 135
Violence. 136
The Final Evening of a Poetry Festival 137

From *The Lions' Gate* (2002)
The Wiles of Odysseus. 141
Of Pikes and Warriors 142

Notes 143

About Titos Patrikios. 145

About the Translators 147

Illustrations

Section pages and endsheets are illustrated with Titos Patrikios's handwritten Greek poems. English titles are listed below.

```
The Lions' Gate (first 9 lines) . . . . . . . . . . . . . Endsheets
Latest News (first 15 lines) . . . . . . . . . . . . . . . . . . . . . 3
Paper . . . . . . . . . . . . . . . . . . . . . . . . . . . . . . . . . . . . 13
Earth and Sea (working draft, first 14 lines) . . . . . . . . 19
Monologue (first 13 lines) . . . . . . . . . . . . . . . . . . . . 39
Carnival Night . . . . . . . . . . . . . . . . . . . . . . . . . . . . 55
Verses, 2 . . . . . . . . . . . . . . . . . . . . . . . . . . . . . . . . . 63
My Hometown . . . . . . . . . . . . . . . . . . . . . . . . . . . 67
Trip . . . . . . . . . . . . . . . . . . . . . . . . . . . . . . . . . . . . 77
Persistence of a City (first 20 lines) . . . . . . . . . . . . . . 95
Secret Life . . . . . . . . . . . . . . . . . . . . . . . . . . . . . . . 99
A Town in Southern Greece . . . . . . . . . . . . . . . . . 117
My Language (first 15 lines) . . . . . . . . . . . . . . . . . 123
Ashes . . . . . . . . . . . . . . . . . . . . . . . . . . . . . . . . . 129
The Wiles of Odysseus (first 20 lines) . . . . . . . . . . . 139
```

Acknowledgments

We gratefully acknowledge Kedros Publishers, Athens, for their permission to translate and publish the poems of Titos Patrikios. We also acknowledge the following journals in which many of our translations of Titos Patrikios's poems were first published or are forthcoming:

Absinthe: New European Writing	"Cold Wind"
	"In the Plunder"
	"Three Dimensions"
	"Tomorrow"
The Atlanta Review	"Catacomb"
The Evansville Review	"Ashes"
Gulf Coast	"The Message"
	"While They Speak"
Literary Imagination	"Carnival Night"
	"Faces"
	"Frame for the Light"
	"Verses, 1"
	"Verses, 2"
Lyric	"The Mountains"
	"The Stone"
Michigan Quarterly Review	"Drafts on Makronissos"
Modern Poetry in Translation	"Via Dei Coronari"
Passport	"Earth and Sea"
	"Elements of Identity"
	"Syllables"
Pleiades	"Monologue"
	"Villa Ariadne"
Poetry Greece	"Cure"
	"The Message"
	"Via dei Coronari 123"
Seneca Review	"Latest News"
	"Open Borders"
Sirena: Poesía, Arte y Crítica	"The Blame"
	"Last Light"
	"Letter"

Tampa Review   "The Lions' Gate"
"Nightmare"
"Trip"
"Besieged Time"
"Flesh"
"Underground Train"
"Via di Tor Millina"

Two Lines   "Cure"

Translators' Preface

This volume includes those poems we consider to be representative of Titos Patrikios's poetic output, beginning with his early poems of detention and including poems from his most recent volumes. Our aim is to give readers in English, especially readers unfamiliar with his work, a means to explore the breadth of his career and to evaluate his achievement. Inevitably, exquisite and perhaps even crucial poems must be neglected in the process of such a "selection." We were fortunate to have a week alone with the Titos Patrikios on the island of Rhodes one December several years ago, and in between alternating cups of coffee and wine, and during walks through the impossibly deserted streets of the old city, we made many of our choices with his gentle guidance. In the end, however, we determined the final contents of this volume and we humbly accept responsibility for any glaring omissions.

This book would not exist without the support of several people and institutions deserving recognition here: The International Writers' and Translators' Centre of Rhodes, Allegheny College, Renna Patrikios, Willis Barnstone, Rachel Hadas, and Kerry Neville Bakken. Thanks to the Benaki Museum, Athens, for the photographs from Mycenae. And thanks, especially, to Titos Patrikios himself, who dedicated many weeks of his life and so much wisdom and hilarity to this project, from Lindos to Athens, and beyond. Our friendship is without doubt the greatest profit of this happy labor.

Introduction

In "Ars Poetica?" Czeslaw Milosz suggests that:

> The purpose of poetry is to remind us
> how difficult it is to remain just one person,
> for our house is open, there are no keys in the doors,
> and invisible guests come in and out at will.

Milosz understood the importance of managing the contentious relationship between human personality and political ideology, not to mention in certain cases the tectonic ordeals of proscription, censorship, and exile. The self is one home, but the homeland is another—both are subject to unsettling visitations. If this volume of poems is any indication, the Greek poet Titos Patrikios also knows the difficulty of remaining one person, as well as the predicament of living in a country haunted by far too many visible and invisible guests.

Patrikios was born in Athens in 1928 to a middle class family of artists and intellectuals. His parents were both actors who traveled widely (including tours in United States in the early 1930s), offering the poet a rather cosmopolitan, if scattered upbringing. He was educated as a lawyer, but through several twists of fate, and because of the turbulent fate of his country, poetry has shaped his existence more than the law. Like many young intellectuals of his time, Patrikios was active in the Communist-led resistance against the German Occupation from 1941 to 1944. As if the noxious presence of the Nazis was not enough, Greeks on the right and left struggled for control of the resistance, exacerbating the already desperate situation in Greece during the occupation, and creating political fractures that led to the civil war that followed. At the end of September 1944, a month before the liberation of Greece, Patrikios was put against a wall in front of a firing squad (composed of fellow Greeks, Nazi sympathizers), but was spared death at the last minute.

Out of the vacuum left by the war, conservative forces from within Greece seized power, and leftists like Patrikios found themselves in a precarious position again, this time with the American and British-backed government of Themistocles Sofoulis, who emerged as prime minister in 1946. Keeping Greece from "going Red" had become a central priority for the Populist leaders of Greece, as well as for the Americans and British. The Communist Party was proscribed in 1947 and in the next several years, around 20,000 Greeks were sentenced for crimes against the state. Many communists, Patrikios included, were forced into political detention on the Greek islands of Makronissos and

Ai-Stratis. The conditions on these islands—Makronissos in particular—were deplorable: prisoners were subjected to torture, solitary confinement, hard labor, and brainwashing. In order to secure their release from detention, prisoners were required to renounce their membership in the Communist Party and sign a document of capitulation and "forgiveness." Despite being tortured and suffering from tuberculosis, which worsened during his detainment, Patrikios never signed.

After Makronissos, Patrikios was transferred to Ai-Stratis, where he met fellow-inmate Yiannis Ritsos, by then an already established literary figure on the left. Ritsos encouraged Patrikios and others to write in spite of their imprisonment; Patrikios's book *Exercises,* for example, consists of surrealist experiments "assigned" to the young poet by his mentor, who would announce a subject ("paper" or "faces") that the detainees would improvise upon during their labor each day. Ritsos edited Patrikios's first manuscripts and their friendship was crucial to Patrikios personally and artistically throughout his years of detention.

The early phase of Patrikios's career is represented in this volume by selections from his early poems and from his books *Dirt Road, Years of the Stone,* and *Litigations*. These poems demonstrate the powerful influence of Ritsos, but also that of Yiorgos Seferis (the most potent voice in Greek poetry at that moment). Both poets served as models for how a young poet in Greece might confront the modern condition from within the inherited mythopoetic currents of their ancient culture. But these poets also carried in them the influence of high European modernism: Seferis was particularly informed by T. S. Eliot, whom he translated into Greek, and both Ritsos and Seferis borrowed certain stylistic techniques from the French symbolists. During his detention on Makronissos, Patrikios recalled secreting away a copy of Baudelaire's "L'Albatross." Two other Greek poets exerted strong influences on his early work: the pessimistic Kostas Karyotakis and the ubiquitous C. P. Cavafy. Whitman and Mayakofksy, he has said, were crucial in shaping his understanding of the role of the poet. Also, Aris Alexandrou brought into Ai-Stratis a copy of Ezra Pound's *Personae,* which caused immense indignation to the supporters of social-realism within the camp. While participating in the assignments offered by Yiannis Ritsos, Patrikios and fellow detainee-poet Kostas Kouloufakos conducted parallel experiments of their own, in secret, under the invisible influence of Pound, thereby bypassing the Greek mentor's authority.

These early poems bear the obvious marks of the poet's imprisonment and detention. Though they are at times as bitter and sardonic as we might expect, they usually maintain a surprising degree of optimism and faith in the ethos of the ancient homeland, and in the truth-wielding potential of language, in spite of an official silencing. In this way, Patrikios will remind readers of two other poets of exile and imprisonment, Nazim Hikmet and Pablo Neruda, poets similarly marked by the tension between celebration and protest, poets more in tune with existential uncertainties than the certitudes of Party praxis. Like Hikmet and Neruda, Patrikios remained more devoted to poetry than to any ideology.

The publication of Patrikios's *Dirt Road* (1954) was viewed as an important moment in Greek letters (the fiftieth anniversary of that publication was recently celebrated with fanfare in Athens). The book consisted of loosely symphonic long poems, like "Earth and Sea," that register what attracted Greek readers to Patrikios's voice early on: a poignant sense of what Greece was losing through a lens of almost surreal pastoral. Though steeped in a landscape of death and the stultifying atmosphere of the prison islands, these poems are ultimately lyrics of positive defiance, rising nearly to Whitmanian heights in "Facing up to the Sky," his homage to Ritsos.

For many Greeks, not just those on the left, the period leading through the Greek Civil War and the decade that followed is one of the darkest in recent cultural memory. Although Patrikios's poems of detention have their specific origins in a nearly forgotten bit of history—the ugliest manifestation of the Cold War in Greece—little historical context is necessary to support them; they offer understated and poignant documentation of a simple fact: the experience of living inside a frail, but resistant human body in extreme human circumstances. The poems from *Dirt Road* and *Years of the Stone* were written simultaneously, and both were forbidden—the poet actually had to bury his manuscripts to keep them from being seized by the authorities. Rather than compose hymns celebrating the unalterable nobility of his comrade detainees, which members of his Party would have preferred, Patrikios dedicated most of these poems to the mundane and undignified facts of camp life, presenting these with a matter-of-fact transparency that rises almost automatically toward irony.

The poems written between 1959 and the mid 1970s (represented by his books *Apprenticeship, Apprenticeship Again, Sea of Promise, Optional Stop,* and *Deformities*) demarcate the next phase of Patrikios's career. Returning to Athens in 1954 as a detainee "on leave," he had become a resolute anti-Stalinist, yet up until 1959 (when his status as a lawyer allowed him to leave the country) he continued being asked to sign documents of capitulation, strangely enough every year on his birthday. From 1959 to 1964, Patrikios studied sociology and philosophy at the Ecole Pratique des Hautes Etudes and at the Sorbonne. In 1964, he returned to Athens to find himself again at odds with his fellow Greeks. By then, Patrikios had become more and more outwardly critical of the Communist Party and its activities around the world, leading finally to a definitive rupture with the Communist Party and also with Yiannis Ritsos, who remained steadfast (at least publicly) in his political allegiance. But the poems from this period also satirized the high rhetoric, pomp and circumstance of artists who agreed to capitulate with the right wing and Patrikios's books were therefore simultaneously rejected by critics from both political extremes.

If the early phase of his career is marked by pastoral imagery and nostalgic lyricism, much of it juxtaposed with the ordeals of his island detention, in his next phase we find Patrikios becoming a primarily urban poet, a writer of short satirical and erotic poems. Many work upon the architecture of mysterious syllogisms, or legal formulas, and most proceed according to the logic of dreams. In 1967, the poet fled to France to escape the military dictatorship of the "Colonels." He spent his exile in Paris and Rome working for UNESCO and various French research institutes. The poet's loss of his home and his mother tongue are clearly evident in these poems, which combine nostalgic recollections of sexual encounter (challenging the reserved style of poetry popular at that moment in Greece) with an almost allegorical longing for what is absent: the body of the beloved woman, as well as the body of the beloved homeland. The brevity and directness of these poems also reflect a difficult ambivalence. Patrikios describes the early 1970s as a kind of "fallow period" for Greek writers; while poets in Greece were essentially "on strike," reluctant to publish under the circumstances demanded of them by the censors, those outside of Greece, like Patrikios, found in their displacement a profound, but guilt-ridden motivation to speak for those who could (or would) not.

Since his return from exile, Patrikios has been awarded the National Prize in Literature from the Greek government in 1992, and he served as the Chairman of the Athens 2004 Cultural Olympiad for one year. Kedros Publishers put out a three-volume *Collected Poems* in 1998. Patrikios has published several volumes since then, including *Opposing Mirrors, The Pleasures of Extension, The Lions' Gate,* and *Resistance of the Facts,* and several books of prose aphorisms. These books were not written in the shadow of foreign monuments, in adopted cities, from a distance; indeed, now Patrikios's book-lined apartment near Kolonaki overlooks a horizon dominated by the Acropolis. But certain tensions still inform his work. The leading Greek critic, Dimitris Maronitis, finds in the poetry of Patrikios several persistent archetypes, foremost among them, "the reinstatement of the outcast in public life," one that is "internally undetermined by the ghosts of dead friends and the memories of a group of people that has completely fallen apart."

As Patrikios himself puts it, in the poem from which we have borrowed the title of this volume:

> Our past is forever full, terrible,
> just as the story of what happened is terrible,
> carved as it is now, written on the lintel
> of the gate we pass through every day.

Here readers in English will finally encounter "the story of what happened," in the voice of a Greek poet courageous enough to pass through the lions' gate again and again, making what he can out of the terrible, sublime history of his country.

Christopher Bakken
Athens, Greece, and Meadville, Pennsylvania, 2006

The Lions' Gate

The lions had already departed.
Not even one in all of Greece,
except for a rather solitary, evasive
lion hiding out somewhere on the Peleponnesus,
a threat to no one at all,
until it too was slaughtered by Hercules.
Still, our memories of lions
never stopped terrifying us:
their terrible images on coats of arms and shields,
their terrible figures on battle monuments,
that terrible relief carved
into a stone lintel over the gate.
Our past is forever full, terrible,
just as the story of what happened is terrible,
carved as it is now, written on the lintel
of the gate we pass through every day.

Early Poems
(1948–1951)

Τελευταῖες εἰδήσεις

Καμινάδες νεκρές, δίχως καπνό
ἄδεια ἀπὸ γέλιο στόματα
καρδιὲς ποὺ νίκησαν καὶ πέθαναν —
πρέπει νὰ γκρεμίσουμε τὰ χείλη τῆς ἀβύσσου.

Ἄνθρωποι, πάνω ἀπ' ὅλα ἄνθρωποι
ἀδιάκοπα, χωρὶς ἀνάσα, χωρὶς ντροπὴ
γυμνοὶ ἀπὸ ἀμφιβολίες
τίποτα κρυμμένο
ἂς ξεκινοῦμε πάλι μὲς στοὺς δρόμους
νὰ χτίσουμε ξανὰ τὴ ζωή,
νὰ χτίσουμε ρεῦτοι ἐμεῖς τὴ ζωή.

Φωτιὲς γεμάτος ὁ οὐρανὸς
κι ἀναποδογυρισμένα σύννεφα
ποὺ τὰ ἐπηρέασε τὸ μουγκρητὸ —
μόλις τὸ πρόλαβαν οἱ ἐφημερίδες
ἐπὶ τῆς πυρκαγιᾶς

The Conquest of Everest

The expedition heading to Tibet
set out one morning quite splendidly;
crowds of people escorted them
to the station, and then to the port,
with twice as many patriotic sermons
and plenty of hurrah
for *our brave boys*.
They were going to the Himalayas
to conquer Everest
and for the glory of the country.
The government offered much assistance,
even bestowed upon them an enormous flag
to erect upon Everest's
untrodden summit.

They had an excellent trip to India
and everything there went just fine
though one thing did grieve them:
a couple of Sherpas hauling
all their luggage and provisions
died in a bottomless gorge.
Alas, the British officer who led the team
affirmed that it was nothing important,
for things like that happen all the time.
When at last they found a panoramic spot,
they saw almost in front of them
the Himalayas rising.
They forgot their labor and grief
stood amazed for awhile,
and then swore
we'll beat them!

They climbed the snowy crags
leaving expanses and rocky scarps behind
till a time came when their hearts
were seized by a severe vertigo.
There was the sight of Everest,
highest mountain in the world.

They climbed, climbed higher and higher
until they camped in a refuge
of ice, higher than any human had been,
but they had more climbing to do.
For the ultimate ascent,
they picked the two strongest among them,
the most tested ones,
two boys full of life
who blazed off toward their goal
as soon as the weather calmed.
The rest watched this through binoculars
and when they saw them stride to the top
they shouted themselves hoarse with joy;
but when the flag was unfurled
they cried in silence.

The two boys began their descent,
but they were hidden in fog, suddenly
    immersed in snow,
till their remote fire could not hold out.
Nothing was left, even, of the flags and
    hurrahs,
proof that they once existed.

December 1943

Latest News

Dead chimneys, smokeless
mouths emptied of laughter,
hearts that won and died—
we must bridge the lips of the abyss.

Humans, above all humans,
persistent, restless, shameless,
without doubt,
hiding nothing,
let's spill out in the streets again
to build life once again,
to build life first.

A sky full of voices
and overturned clouds
that were executed this noon—
the newspapers got this bit of news
just as they went to print.
Not one of them wrote of the fountains
that opened upon their tortured bodies.

The Friends

It's not the memory of murdered friends
that tears me apart now.
It's the mourning for thousands of unknown others
who left for the beaks of birds
their extinguished eyes,
those who clasp in their cold hands
a clutch of shell casings and thorns.
For the unknown passerby
to whom we never spoke a word,
with whom we only exchanged a glance
when they gave us a light from their cigarette
in the evening street.
For the thousands of unknown friends
who gave their lives
for mine.

19 January 1949

Open Borders

*Remember how we underlined the
same thing in that book by Marx…*

For us there are no long strolls
along streets covered over with trees;
the best we can do is a sidewalk lined with dusty laurels.
In our empty pockets no stars jingle,
just a packet of the cheapest cigarettes
and change from a one-thousand banknote.
At last the foreign consulates measured it,
the newspapers wrote about it in sepia,
the Political Economy Department at the university ignored it:
in our land
we have per capita
eighty dollars a year.

Oh, Acropolis
ancient marbles looking at me,
who passed here,
who fought,
who engraved their names,
who remained unknown for ever…
I'm one of them too.
I step on that same earth
where the illegal books were buried
with the machine guns we stole from the enemy.
I live in the same town
that spreads beyond borders and time.
And all become one,
the dissimilar and the distant.

Hey you, states lying close to me,
I'm speaking to you from Athens

wreathed by a senile sky
that's grown bored with being azure,
the *Red morning sky* of us all.
Paris, I'm talking to you,
with your old guillotines, cobblestones
washed by the rain, the blood,
the abuses of comrades,
Paris without a Seine for suicides.
For you, holy Petrograd,
with the defeated Winter Palace,
you that undressed your name
to put on the humble uniform of Lenin.
I'm talking to you, Madrid,
coal just like us,
run through by Moorish bayonets.
Beloved Madrid, barricade of our own.

Falling somewhere but always winning.
The Battle March.

January 1950

Fires

Stone piled upon more stone
humid stone
stone walls
stone life
in the underground passages
we forgot the light.
Overhead, fires are lit
at the crossroads where they burn our dead.

Tavern "Abundance"

Memories of songs that went old in two, three years
woke from that gramophone in the street,
the antique gramophone with the great horn.
The people who love us did not forget us.

From *Exercises*
(1952)

Χαρτί

Ἕνα ξεχυμένο χαρτί γιά ὀμπρέλα στή βροχή
ἕνα τσαλακωμένο χαρτί γιά καρδιά μές στούς ἀνθρώπους.
Ὅ,τι κι ἄν κάνω μέ τρομάζει
μά ὅ,τι δέν κάνω πιό πολύ μέ βασανίζει.
(Μοιραζόμαστε τόν πόνο μέ τά πράγματα
ὅπως τά στραγάλια στό πανηγύρι τῆς Ἁγα-Μαρίνας.)
Ἕνα χαρτί πού πέταξα στό βροχινό πεζόδρομο
καί τώρα πάνω στό γόνατο τό σιώνω
νά στρώσει σάν πουκάμισο σιδερωμένο
ὅσο κι ἄν ἔσβησε γιά πάντα
ἐκείνη ἡ τυχαία λέξη
πού εἶχα γράψει μέ μελανί μολύβι.

Faces

The earth's face is soggy again.
Walking
in mud up to the knee, up to the belly,
dozing a bit
in deserted churches, in empty schools,
and setting out again
before dawn washes her eyes.

Gushing rivers
we had to cross
while you thought about the flowerpots
left unwatered,
worried when it would rain again
since the water would wash away those tin pots,
and the old flowers you threw in the stream,
since, as you used to say,
such things shouldn't remain in the bedroom
while you are sleeping.
In these places
not even one bridge remains
and if the rain taps on your windows there,
here it taps on our faces.

Thousands of us passed by
marking the earth's face with our boots.
How could the village kids know each one of us.
They run behind awhile, singing along with us
till we disappear again into the woods.
Someday the schools will open,
the big cold classrooms,

young Rinio;
oh, I wish I could fill up your pockets with candies,
young Rinio
with the wooden shoes.

It's time I opened my hand
and let spill
this handful of dirt
on the limitless face of the earth.

Paper

Ordinary paper spread open
for an umbrella against the rain—
a crumpled paper for a heart among people.
Whatever I do scares me,
but whatever I don't do tortures me more.
(We share our pain with things
like the dried chickpeas at the fair of Agia Marina.)
A paper I tossed into the gutter;
now here on my thigh I smooth out
its creases as if ironing a shirt,
though that arbitrary word
you had written there in pen
has been permanently erased.

From *Dirt Road*

(1952–1954)

Earth and Sea

The signs made it obvious early.
Sudden downpours, the sudden anger of the sea,
the horses and oxen on the hillside
looking west and smelling the air…
It's been a long time since the planting.
The peasants drink some raki, rub their numb fingers,
talking about the cold, poverty, the crops,
and then quickly head back home.
About the crops—
and we were talking about the harvest
(besides, there was always somebody to point out the signs),
we too were talking about the soil and the wheat
and the covered pit where the compost ripened.…

•

Upon the cracked window the trees and lightning branch
each time the rain ignites its flashlight.
And the dogs, again the dogs bark at night,
as rain sweeps toward the sea past the sheep pens.
We too were talking about horses—
but about which bare trees were you asking me
behind mother's back,
about which origin of the wind behind the promontory?
I don't remember, I don't remember well.
Now I have two red flames
tacked to my eyes.
Ah, yes. I have to tell you:
it's been months now that the caïque
has been broken on the beach,
and nobody needs it.

•

Always a caïque carries the fervor of our seventeenth year.
When the smoke of acetylene light spreads its sulphur scent
into the corner of changing streets.
Fresh cypress wood,
a caïque—
the sailors have wide salty soles,
broad shoulders wet
from the waves and the spray of summer
and they always chart a course toward home or departure
between the sun and the North Star.
Cypress wood that smells of seas and forests.
Our engine speeds up to nine knots.
At night the waters are phosphorescent,
tattooing the landscape of the stars on our arms
and on the keel.
Nine knots.

•

This year's winter hit hard,
with severe cold, much poverty.
Sometimes it's a bit milder.
Old women run to break off a plank for the fireplace
and then sleet, again sleet and wind.
And old rib cage remains,
the wood whitens like bone.
The amputated arms
rest on the seabed
without nails or flesh on the tips of the fingers,
wrapped up in an old piece of burlap,
shuddering every time
they are brushed by seaweed or a passing octopus.

•

Below the lantern
flows a brook,
below the brook
the rain lies face down
and sleeps.

•

My boy, this picture doesn't look like you anymore.
You were a deer that knew all the secret sources of water,
all the huts of the woodsmen in the clearings of the forest.
(Two tears in the corners of her eyes
like two anchors in the eyes of a ship.)
My deer, you had a forehead mother caressed,
two little hands you plunged into the big pocket of her
    overcoat.
(Two tears lost
and forgotten.)

•

Ah, mother, you knew we would read until morning,
forgetting and ignoring the doctor who slowly folded his
    stethoscope,
saying, *sleep before midnight has double value.*
And turning on the x-ray machine he would repeat:
rest, above all rest and peace of mind.
You knew and you didn't speak.
You only stayed awake
waiting for the strip of light and smoke
that slipped under our doors
to be snuffed out.
Mother, mother,

deep inside you knew there would not be any rest,
you knew our gaze was abandoning you,
lurking behind your shoulders when you
hugged us and when you did not.
You knew that we would leave,
that we would be leaving.
You heard about the sea and the land,
keeping silent and wondering how others
returned early and wisely in the evening
to eat soup all together with the family.
Ah, how you were jealous without loving them,
and you, your smile quietly enclosed within two brackets
    of bitterness,
spying on us so we wouldn't see you and be angry.

•

You were afraid and enjoyed
our greedy look that every day discovers and becomes
    enriched
experiencing the history of the world from the beginning.
Mother, mother, you leaned from the balcony when we
    were late
and scanned the street;
in our love,
beyond our love,
there is another love
wild and uncompromising and tender
with a face scratched and bleeding
from the chase and the wires,
howling and starving for a future.

•

Beneath the light
there is a brook.
Behind our sorrow
there is a flower.
If we grab the wrist of night
we'll touch the pulse of time,
its fever and its health.
If we put our ear to the earth
we will hear the loud panting,
the lost rivers that always exist,
seeking to find the passage that connects
the soil with the sea.

Our earth.
Having contractions,
preparing.

•

The caïque has broken; and the low wall where at sunset
we set down our thoughts and some sweets, it's crumbled;
the cow has died—
but no matter what happens
it's always the sea that retracts and verifies,
it's the soil taking and giving back,
it's the seed of summer that feeds winter's heart.

•

We traveled a lot,
by ships, by trains, by trucks.
In the pulley block of our heart
howls the ceaseless rope of moments and landscapes.
Hard is the journey,
dear and long,

very long, mother.
Wipe from the windows for a moment the downpour of
    centuries
and see how long it lasts.
Beneath the tree rings of the clouds
pass by and depart
so many triremes, and caravels, and barges,
so many legions that did not perish
but live within us.

•

Mother,
when you don't see us
just know that we went out to welcome you.
When our houses lose us, they should know that we went
to look for the cement they require.
When life stops by and doesn't ask where we are,
tell life that some dawn on a certain hill she will find us.
Only one favor, mother: love even those you didn't love.
Love even those you loved, but forgot you.
Love us.

•

This year's winter hit hard.
With famine and flood and fatalities.
(The signs—
we have always seen them but we didn't care.)
Even without us
the sun never stops its journey.
The soil gives and takes life back,
and death is a fertilizer.
Hard winter—
ah, we hope in this winter,

don't expect anymore a relapse of the summer that has
    passed.
That was healed and is gone.

•

Yes, tacked to my eyes
there are two red flames.
Behind them people are seen more clearly.
They seem humane.
We won't have any other profit, mother.
There won't be any rewards, or fame, or applause.
Only love.
Love that leads and guides, but makes no promises.

Mother, what are you looking for in our faces?
If our faces take on a sunburned shade
you didn't expect, it is because we
were burned for your own good.

•

The journey, long and dear.
Still, before one's love for the journey,
comes grain for the people,
which has to descend from the broad plains
to be ground and become bread.
Proceeding down time's endless dirt road,
we came across the ruts from other carts.
(How many half-buried dreams in the hardened mud,
stepped upon; how many erected as milestones to show the
    way....)

One by one the carts return to the villages,
disappear in the mist of the past.

Now only our cart is there to take the grain
to the mill.
Yes, we too talk about horses,
we inscribe new lines on the dirt road
that's expecting our traces.
We set up our dreams on the road signs of history.

•

Mother, the journey is long.
But the earth and the sea do not separate us,
they cannot separate us.
The earth is gentle with its winters, with forests,
large cities, fields, factories…
The sea is gentle with the cruise ships,
with the schools of eels searching for the gates of the rivers,
with rowboats in small harbors, with squalls,
with birds combing her wild hair…
Look at the children drawing them
with a thick, dark blue marker.
The earth and the sea, mother,
they unite people.

December 1952–March 1953

Facing Up to the Sky

—for Yiannis Ritsos

From stone to stone, from root to root, from lamp
to lamp, the night shivering, like a glass ear of wheat,
leads back to that other vegetation
which now, beneath our bodies, is coal
for the dense, reverse wells of the stars
as they heave the buckets of their distant fire.
A word, another word, a gesture, a thousand mouths
in every posture, in every movement, the girlish laughter
you had only foreseen, deep violin silence,
a circle closing, a continuing chain
and the open veins of time without end or beginning.

Four faces grope the sky:
Vega—the swooping eagle;
Altair—the rising eagle
(over the narrow valleys we set out from);
and Cassiopeia, exquisite Cassiopeia,
in spite of strict Athena, and the sand covering them all.
All alone—remember?—Andromeda scared too, on the beach,
having heard nothing from Perseus
and still hoping.
The roads of the stars, the human roads,
the plains of the universe fluted with crisscrossing lines,
endless millions of light years...

And, so what?

II

Sky, do you think we're content just looking at you?
It seems to me you don't know us.

No matter how often you repeat your well-meant romances,
interject the soggy bellies of the clouds,
or sometimes extrude down to
naked grain the final future,
we need to find you, original,
past each decrepit countenance,
we can find you, we can teach you
what you are, but you ignore
or forget it.
Don't clench your jaws, Sky,
don't become angry or fear us,
we won't do more harm to you than is necessary.
We can save you.

The footsteps of stars that tread upon so many strong bodies
and so many corpses
are welcomed in our hearts.
Their rays that saw away at the earth's crust
are welcome too.
But they should know.
We keep going,
we blow up the corners of every sun that blocks
our path,
we put our foot on the neck of any constellation impeding us.
And these rotten stars
with their cold, empty carcasses,
facades with pretensions of light,
need a good cleaning.

III

In the harsh loneliness of brine,
in the muscular movements of oceans
inhabited only by silence,

life was being prepared
as in every fragment of light colors are prepared.

Life in the guts of the granite and the atmosphere,
life in the ragged underwear of sleep,
life over the ashes, life under the snow,
and there, in the middle, erect, masculine
with his unshaven Byzantine face,
Death—
a pause reconnecting the motion,
a well-made boot exhausting the limits of comfort,
a garment covering the chilled shadow of the moon,
a table set by life for her food,
metal on the edge of a leaf at the beginning of the forest.
Through fountains and fountains, from savagery to savagery,
from lovemaking to lovemaking, from grave to grave,
and cook pot to cook pot, a wave surges.
A wave calls out, a wave searches, denudes your flesh,
denudes the wave, unearths bones from the petrified light,
turns death upside down, broadens life,
and cripples it, makes it stronger—but what is it after?
Where does the wave go? Where do we go? Where do we go?

We press on.

And you, Sky, having watched over the endless recycling
of life and death
the world growing up, humans growing tall,
having seen all the hungry,
all the tortured,
all the persecuted,
don't forget:
beyond the grumbling
there's victory.

And all this little life of ours
doesn't accept death.

IV

It doesn't accept death, it doesn't accept death
it doesn't accept death, but you are not a cell
ignoring its ending, you are not a deer
trembling with fear, going dumb—you know it
and you choose it and you don't want it and you don't want it.
However, from weariness and from love, from the wooden plow
    of wasted time,
from the worn out banknotes of words,
from the legs of a chair that still stands in the craters of poverty,
from the man with the Panama hat, from the barefoot wheat of rain,
from the holes of the sun, from the stone and the soap,
from the steps that keep track of your steps,
death is coming
like a hand reaching for bread, like trains reaching
the curtains of night.
Death is coming—Yiorgi, Yiorgi.
A sea of blood is covering us at night—
Yiorgi...
On our faces, in our mouths, in our nostrils—
a sea of blood.
Yiorgi, do you hear me?
We, who an hour ago didn't know one another—
bring your faces closer
lighten up, lighten up
bring your faces, bring the fire, bring your voices.
Do you hear me? Do you all hear me?
It doesn't strangle us, it doesn't exhaust us—
Hello...hello...do you hear me?

No, I'm not the radio that restores silence,
I only spit out the last ember of night;
we should only hurry up, hurry up.
Speak up, speak up.
I'm all right, I'm telling you, I'm all right,
we are together.

Bring your hands, bring the fire.
It doesn't accept death, it doesn't …

V

I'll never be able to become again
a block of silent copper.
I'll never be able to forget
all the faces of those who forgot themselves.
I'll never be able to breathe again in an air
not broadened by thousands and thousands of lives.

This rock is my home too,
and those fig trees
are also my homeland,
but only one color above my eyes,
only one vein of spring below my earth,
only an epoch within me:
it's not enough.
I want my land in full, I want the tired man
to bear so much death and so much sun;
I want thousands of houses with their fireplaces lit
or with their fireplaces toppled; I want the hoe,
and the spade and the nets,
the forehead bleeding sweat
oh my tortured hope,
oh my earth, my earth, my country,

hold me tightly in your arms
and let me weep, weep, weep
for every murdered gorge of yours, for every
orphaned island, for every famished field,
let me cry deeper than your roots,
more bitterly than your mourning
more certain than your light—
until I am reborn with you.
I want the noise of the machines,
the warm scent of the body,
I want our voice.

Speak up, speak up!
I'm leaving you, Yiorgi, I'm leaving every friend,
for Agapi, we'll be sacrificing even love.
Now that we've met, we separate.
I have to go where I'm friend to no one,
where nobody wants me to be.

VI

Nights with their doors latched tight,
in the safety of a filthy bed,
in the dream that forgets those footsteps that trample darkness,
a tired dream, dumb, with only semen, with only saliva,
for a moment shutting up the fractured howls
and again in the heat of greed and nudity.
Days with the rust of tears hidden well,
in dark, brand new suits,
days trapped by the self-earned bread,
and then, when the feast is over,
the port guard who oversees the transport of its bones.
And from good morning to good morning, from silence to silence,
the fear—
as from death to death only half a cigarette lapses.

Where I was denied and will be denied again,
forgotten, ignored, a bothersome, obsolete acquaintance,
a mask eaten away by terror and ice,
as change stands out before the fear of change,
where I was turned away and spit upon, where I was smiled upon,
and then they hid behind the chimneys of the future
even if it was all about the weekend with their fiancées,
and I was left alone, my arm outstretched, in the middle of
    deserted autumns,
a wind only pushing salt deeper into wounds opened by kisses,
where we starved together and now I'm not part of their hunger,
where we ate together and now I'm not given bread and coal
where we walked and now I'm refused the step and the stone
where we slept and now I'm refused the sleep and the hope
where we lived and now I'm refused even the door of their house
where we didn't live and now I'm refused security and patience—
I'll go there.

Because there exists in everyone something that is not lost
there is something in everyone that life grips firmly with both hands.

VII

From the badly plastered walls of dusk,
from oil, from the kitchens of poor houses,
from the orphanage, from shorn peasant boys of the stars
life never stops coming, like a deluge
of flags and wheat.
(A fish with the most incredible memory, our eyes
swimming in the clenched veins of the sky.)

You love marble, you love clay, the aged
freedom of trees, the elements and their compounds,
all the geometry of the stars—
you don't love in order to love

but to take your love further.
You love life.

You love movement, a blind insect, an animal
that lost you on the other side of time,
you love all of the dirt road we crossed.
You love the human being.

A sadness, a spring widening the curves of the lips,
two knotty hands, forgotten,
you meet and love the man
so as to glean drop by drop
seed by seed
stone by stone
action by action
his real face
the one scattered between pollen and rivers
the one lost among furniture and cinemas.

They run, they run, with sobs bunched in their arms,
with what the wind left over to satisfy their hunger,
with some rags of truth to deceive the cold—
no, I won't be able to see in each person
the fluid metal of clasped hands,
a life worn out by life.

We have to move on.

VIII

Barbed wire of stars, islands tied hand and foot,
mud, exile, stone through the cracks of nails
flooding the heart, cold, exile,
again rain from the lifted flap of the tent,
a paper that adds one year, and another year,
another paper useful for nothing now,

books dug to the bone, a shared life
people so tortured, so conscious of love,
love exists, doesn't exist, a bitter thorn
erect in the mouth,
a letter that's not coming, a letter that comes when
nobody else receives any, time gained,
unemployed time, the rage of unemployed time, rage of knowledge,
rage of moving on, even within the barrier of redundant winters,
more people, more tortured joy.
My twenty-five years cramped in decades
of persecutions and deprivations—
no, I won't do you the favor of growing used to you, getting
    comfortable.
I don't adapt to death.

And you, cut out that smile of idiotic optimism.
It doesn't suit us.
Just drag the pieces of your lips along the blood,
all the blood, blood from wounds, spit blood,
from scattered bowels, from abortions,
from delayed transfusion bottles,
from murdered truths,
from mutilated children—
dye it in the bitterness and trust,
dye it in a new optimism hammered out by the present.

IX

With the health
of a permanently vanquished illness,
uprooting, uprooting every legend
and through those lacerated myths
the new history breathes,
beyond small, individual loves,
a cascade of worldwide brotherhood.

That great scaffolding of knowledge
keeps approaching, Sky.
With a single kick
poetic nightstands disappear
from the sides of your sickbed.
Yeah, we'll make you feel better.
we'll clean you up like a huge shop window
from the dust of centuries.

So come with us, comrade Sky
revitalized,
come the way the future comes
through the demolished riverbanks
of fear and death.
Come, come.
Come.

On a night like this
four faces take shape more clearly:
Yiorgis, Vasilis, Karolos, and myself.
On a night like this
there's something new.
A new friend,
a new beat in the heart of tomorrow,
a window open wide to happiness.
Alcor, Alcor, double star…
Oh, in this life of ours
there's space for you, space for the whole clamshell of the sky.

Hoping, hoping.

On a night like this
you hear the tread of the world
as it moves on.

Ai-Stratis, December 1953

From *Years of the Stone*
(1953–1954)

Μονόλογος

Ξερριζώνω τὶς λέξεις μία-μία
ἀπ' τὸ λαρύγγι μου.
Ἂν στάζουν αἷμα
τύλιξ'τες στὸ μαντήλι σου
τύλιξ'τες μὲ μπαμπάκι
ἢ πάλι πιάσε τις μὲ τὴ λαβίδα
καὶ πές:
«Ἔτσι τὰ λέει,
γιὰ ἐντύπωση».
Κάνε ἐπιτέλους ὅ,τι δεῖ.
Ὅμως δὲ ἐτάνει πιὰ ἡ σιωπή
δὲ ἐτάνουν πιὰ τὰ λόγια.
Ξερριζώνω μ[ία] [μ]ιά σιωπή λέξει

Drafts on Makronissos

I

With your wind that picks up at night,
with your night that swells the silence
and with barbed wire around your heart.

Island, no earthquake
will swallow you,
stretched like a compass needle of stone
indicating both north and south
of our course
of history
of time.

And the sea flows and goes,
flows and goes,
cannot stand these rocks,
flows and goes.

II

BETO, AETO, CETO, SFA, the Gamma Center,
stone from head to toe,
the pup tents like muddy clods,
and the men pieces of mud,
the soul flickered, became dirt,
ghostly lamps clipped the faces,
lighting the eyes of madmen,
mouths pouring out insects
and the wind with a torturer's heavy boots
whips the jagged mountain with its army belt.

III

Thick worms from the barrack latrines,
giant rats from the cesspools
dig all night into loaves, backpacks,
creep over faces,
the half-eaten face of a cat.
Like a crow, day perches on the mountain
and night falls where the privates masturbate,
night with patrols, with loaded guns.
Behind the latrines
two in lewd acts, in moonlight—
one had a wife and kids.
And a certain Skarvellas
poking his rotten mug into my sleep
to see if I am singing.

IV

Drunks walked on muddy paths
and the old partisan sang, with sobs and spit,
Embros ELAS yia teen Ellada
until he was busted by the MPs.
Sophianos was crawling next to me,
stinking of ouzo, crying in the empty barracks:
I am a snitch, I became a snitch
for a forty-eight hour leave,
shove me away, shove me...
And I was holding his head up
so he could puke.

V

That's how I learned how heavy sandbags are,
how unbreakable stone can be,
how to uproot shrubs and brambles.
The sand remained in my mouth forever,
stone forever in my heart,
the thorns forever stuck under my nails.

March 1953–December 1954

Another Day in Ai-Stratis

The sun rose against even this edge of ours,
a brand new day
washed long ago in the orchards of our village
by bare-armed girls of marrying age.

A promise of summer also rose,
a promise for the great trees
which will expand with morning branches
and fill the square with rustling and shade,
even grow beyond the boats,
when we've become old
and we'll be loving from a distance.

A horizon also rose
to suspend in its arms the mountain
with its crystallized eons and crystallized snow,
looking at us calmly and looking without nodding.
And the boats—so red,
and drying so quickly after the rough sea.
And the sand
drying too after the gushing rivers.
But which rough seas
do the old men in cafes contemplate,
which seas....

Why wouldn't they want to stroll with unexpected
    company...
No, don't say if you know,
don't think you can know.
Just listen to the girls from our village,
those with bare arms

who take down one by one from the lines
the days of tomorrow, freshly washed,
and tuck them into a large trousseau,
tossing in two bundles of lavender
against moths
and oblivion.

Frame for the Light

Come to your window unnoticed by your mother
and pretend you're watering the marjoram…
—Folk Song

Neither a mother here, nor a caress,
nor sweet talk, the words
arrive changed at their destination,
don't arrive, don't start out at all, remain
nailed to the walls, drying like octopus.
Neither a mother, nor a flowerpot to water,
brackish water, salty air, the faces
assume a statuelike aspect as the flesh
is fused with salt—
but you would still come to your window in the mornings
wrapped in the warm glare of sleep
and through your rose-colored nightgown
a stream of light poured upon the thirsty day.

Such extravagance of light—perhaps you guessed
that your endurance was running out.

Military March

The stars grow angry and foam at the mouth
like an epileptic private
who had a fit during the drills.
Whether he faked it or not…
Anyhow, he did not get away with it
by going to the infirmary.
We'll never get away
if we get sick or if we flee.

I wanted to tell it to the person next to me,
but he was chanting a military march.

Monologue

I uproot the words one by one
from my throat.
If they are leaking blood,
wrap them in a handkerchief,
wrap them up in cotton
or snatch them with tweezers
and say:
He's just talking
to impress.
Well, do whatever you like.
But silence is not enough anymore;
talk is not enough either.
One by one I uproot plain words
and send them to you.

Verses, 1

Verses, like children.
Inside the guts they grow with secret noises.
They are in pain inside you, they get sick,
then grow up unexpectedly;
one day they revolt against you
who gave birth to them,
until one day they leave for good
and cease to belong only to you.

Habits of the Detainees

Every morning the sun rises behind the guardhouses
wearing filthy hospital pajamas,
crossing slowly the courtyard of the sky.

After so many years
it too has taken up the habits of the detainees.

Syllables

And what I am left with from your passing
little by little is battered by time
like a river pebble.
I'm only certain about your name.
And I keep saying it, again and again, facing the sea
just in case some night,
when we're strangled by wires and stone,
I need it as a word of salvation
and discover suddenly that too is gone.

Plaster Sky

Your garters are still on the bedpost
and the comb from your hair is on the floor.

Through the old window
the plaster of the sky was falling.

Night in the Tent

> *The bread and the knife lie down like brothers...*
> ——Costas Koulafakos

From the upper window the moon's marble dust falls slowly,
whitens the grime of the kerosene stove,
gives to a cardboard box its original shine,
as when it first arrived as a parcel,
erases wrinkles from the faces of the comrades,
makes them smooth again as when they first joined the movement...
These people and things lie down like brothers;
only the crackle of the canvas is heard
as it rots, as the tent, death and sleep constantly rot—
it's time to rain at last, for everything to become mud,
with no illusions, to be reborn through the mud
if they can, in the light.

From *Litigations*
(1955)

Βράδυ ἀποκριᾶς

Μέσα στὸ σκοτεινὸ κελὶ
μὲ λύσσα ἐπιθυμοῦσα ἕνα δέντρο, ἕνα πρᾶγμα ζωντανό.
Στοὺς μουχλιασμένους τοίχους βούλιαζε τὸ βλέμμα μου
σ' ἀπηγχονισμένους ἀποχαιρετισμούς, σ' ὀνόματα ἐκτε-
 λεσμένων
ποῦ μπερδεύονταν μαζὶ μὲ τὸ σούβλα
σὰ νὰ τοὺς ξανασκότωναν μὲς στὰ γέλια καὶ τὶς
 φυσαρμόνικες
τῶν ἀνίδεων μασκαράδων ποὺ πέρναγαν στὸ δρόμο.
Ἀκόμα δὲν εἶχα καταλάβει πῶς ἡ φυσοδέχτη ἀπὸ μέσα
κι οἱ δεσμοφύλακες τίποτα δὲν μποροῦσαν νὰ μοῦ πάρουν.

While They Speak

While they speak in cafes
of love and freedom and that kind of thing,
how could you say love was abandoned,
how it eluded even solitude,
or how justice is shaped by the chaos
of a thousand insults and errors;
how could you say that freedom
could only be attained in the bottom of crowded cells
where all the hours of our lives are held captive.

Carnival Night

In the dark cell
I had a mad craving for a tree, for a living thing.
My gaze penetrated the moldy walls,
desperate goodbyes, names of the executed
crumbling with the plaster,
as if they'd been shot again among the laughter
    and harmonicas
of ignorant revelers passing in the street.
I hadn't yet realized that nature began in me
so the guards could take nothing away.

Last Light

How can you go into this deranged night?
The last light is being held like a blade.
How will you face winter
clinging to a few days from last summer?
There's a corpse stretched before your eyes.
There's a shattered corpse in your clothes.
In the early morning, street cleaners stuff
rags in the potholes opened by kisses.

Tomorrow

Flesh, desire, the body's inner surfaces,
where into cells your first ideas slip.
You don't know what it means to deny
   them all for tomorrow.

Three Dimensions

The kisses abandon his body in panic
sensing that death approaches,
like a slew of rats
jumping ship before it sinks.

With the waning motion of one who is dying
he turns the kisses away from his face
like flies storming the nostrils and mouth,
like those black flies that sniff out death.

So those kisses stuck and rooted in his body,
where they remain even after his death
and keep on growing
like fingernails.

Flesh

My flesh
always hurts when beaten,
always rejoices when caressed.
It hasn't learned a thing.

From *Apprenticeship*
(1956–1959)

Στίχοι, 2

Στίχοι πού κραυγάζουν
στίχοι πού ὀρθώνονται τάχα σὰν ξιφολόγχες
στίχοι πού ἀπειλοῦν τὴν καθεστηκυῖα τάξη
καὶ μέσα στοὺς λίγους τόδες τους
κάνουν ἢ ἀνατρέπουν τὴν ἐπανάσταση,
ἄχρηστοι, ψεύτικοι, κομπαστικοί,
γιατὶ κανένας στίχος σήμερα δὲν ἀνατρέπει καθολικὰ
κανένας στίχος δὲν κινητοποιεῖ τὴ μάχη.
(Ποιὰ μάχη; Μεταξύ μας τώρα —
ποιοὶ σύρονται τὴ μάχη;
Τὸ πολύ μια λύτρωση ἀτομική, ἂν ὄχι ἀνάδειξη.)
Γι' αὐτὸ κι ἐγὼ δὲ γράφω πιὰ
γιὰ νὰ προσθέτω χάρτινα ντουφέκια
ὅπλα ἀπὸ λόγια φλύαρα καὶ μούφα.
Μόνο μιὰν ἄκρη τῆς ἀχτίδας νὰ σηκώσω
νὰ ῥίξω λίγο φῶς στὴν φωτογραφημένη μας ζωή.
Ὅσο μπορῶ, κι ὅσο κρατήσω.

Αὔγουστος, 1957

Verses, 2

Verses that howl,
verses that stand stiff as bayonets,
verses that threaten the established order
and with a few feet
cause or overthrow a revolution,
are useless, phony, arrogant,
since no verse today overthrows regimes,
no verse mobilizes the masses.
(What masses? Between us now—
who cares about the masses?
The most verses give is some individual
redemption, if not notoriety.)
That's why I don't write anymore
just to offer paper rifles,
guns made of verbose and hollow words.
Only to lift up the very edge of truth,
to shed a little light
on our fraudulent lives.
As long as I can, as long as I can hold out.

August 1957

From *Apprenticeship Again*
(1959–1962)

To Learn

When you finally find out
how many illusions you had maintained,
when you are forced to recognize
even those things you didn't want to admit,
when the last idol supporting
your beliefs tumbles,
then you may start to learn
how deep and how dark
go the roots of all your deeds.

                                    Paris, November 1959

My Hometown

I touch the walls of the houses,
no one responds.
I find myself in a nameless town.
I search the sky to find its position
but am blinded by colorful signs.
My hometown had two simple orientations:
north latitude, blood
east longitude, death.

Elements of Identity

And the comedy resumed each time the curtain fell,
each time I thought the show had ended.
In my modest costume,
remnants of paint on my face,
colorful rags beneath my overcoat,
no more than a joker whose only use
is as a harmless treatment for indigestion
with his caustic, inconsequential truths,
with his odd words and manners,
with bunches of bats hidden
in the empty dome of his heart.
What would be the use of open debate,
of my screams outside windows shut tight?
It was hard to balance
through the storm in which we found ourselves,
with a life flowing among hoards of the dead
and those underground meetings.

Judge not, lest you be judged.
Prosecute not, lest you be prosecuted.
Ridiculous words for days like these,
as if you'd told me poems
played a central role in class conflict.
We used to judge and were judged always,
prosecute and prosecuted, until
the police, gentlemen, inscribed me in their files
    indelibly,
the revolution, comrades, inscribed me in its own
    indelibly,
and I was left naked in the end beneath the
    spotlights of others;
my actions acquired a different meaning

in the balance of forces
in which I was a small part;
my words were distorted to fit the aims
accepted by me. So how can I speak now,
how judge, or be judged, without causing damage,
without receiving praise from those I hate?
And the stone's sleep will not end,
the moon's tongue will not be quenched.
Have I gone completely blind
here in this cell where I spent my years?
Have I compromised by refusing to compromise?
Have my veins gone dry
being sure of what will come?
Have my words become petrified
getting ready for the Thirtieth Congress?
Have my own crops withered
while struggling to increase agricultural production?
Have my ideas gone dry while responsibly
    discussing
the sound construction of socialism?

Perhaps love is dead for me
in its definite form:
respect for another, fear of myself?
And now behind your backs I laugh
secretly spitting into my handkerchief
purulent and acrid verses?
Or perhaps none of this existed at all,
perhaps I never experienced any of this,
and I simply invent, inflate, dramatize
in the habit of a poet?
Perhaps a wave lifted me up
and crashed me…

I never spoke of what I've done,
mute in my conspiratorial arrogance,
never spoke of my obsolete heroism,
so obsolete it cannot change
my present quiet life—
quiet water, what do you hide in your mire;
flesh, assailing me, death,
silent bird, with your erect wings
keeping the rhythm of my night;
sun, with your incendiary grenades
around my meat like barbed wire;
what are you all hiding?
So, suffocate me or not, I am here,
relapsing endlessly, recovering unexpectedly,
with a modest position in the revolution,
in literature, in society,
an element so persistent, disruptive and
    unrepentant,
I cannot determine if it is
loyalty to the movement or the fear of banishment
that gives my words a kind of balance,
laudable for some and disgraceful for others.

January 1961

Eight Years

Away eight years.
Prison, Makronissos, exile.
When he returned,
the friends would embrace him and ask.
But what he said seemed too simple,
so ordinary...
And he shut his eyes for a moment
to see again the freezing isolation,
those nights in the ravine,
to relive a little the agonies of each day,
which now, in the sated city,
turned into common redundancies.

A Family Lunch

Again we sat at the table, the three of us.
From time to time, he would imagine it
and then his face cast a strange shadow.
Mother, her eyes red from secret tears,
looked as if she was meeting him for the first time
and desperately refused to believe it.
I knew for a long time now that he would die
and I had to be cool until my guts froze.
All three of us wanted to do something else
at last, to reveal something awful that would not
be forgotten. But as always we began our lunch
chatting, nagging, laughing,
making plans for the future,
as on thousands of other days, which had just then
become a slight, fleeting smudge of time.

The Door

The poet was explaining the secret symbolism,
the dialectics of his poem.
The door, he said, is the mystery of communication,
the inner with the outer, a communication that is
alternated, reversed, restrained,
refuted, that relapses, finally occurs,
and that's why the door is a door
that consumes the door,
thaat exceeds the necessity of door,
and through that self-negated door
might someone fathom, *frathom,*
fratathom, flutothum...
All around his admirers felt a deep dew
as they were sprayed with saliva.

From *Sea of Promise*
(1959–1963)

Ταξίδι

Έσπαγα τὸ κορμί σου σὰ ζαχαροκάλαμο
σὲ κάθε κόμπο κάθε λεθρωση
ρουφώντας ἀπὸ τῆ ρωγμὴ χυμό.
Κι ἰσὺ διαρκῶς ἀναδυόσουν πιὸ ἀκέρια
μὲ σκέπαζες μὲ τὴν πολύβουη ἐμύλωσιά σου
τὴν δροσερὴ δροσιὰ τῆ θαλασσινὴ σου νύχτας
καὶ μὲ ταξίδευες ὅλο τὸ δρόμο
ἀπὸ τὸ ἀζεῖμι ὣς τὸν ἄνθρωπο.

Σίφνος, Αὔγουστος 1959

Cure

For one moment a skein of sun will encompass everything
and all will be cured beneath the blaze of your eyes.
Even the scent of your body heals.

Athens, May 1959

The Blame

A sure solution is flesh:
a forgiveness extorted
for an inexcusable blame,
a blame that will return.
And beneath those dark embraces
the abyss of routine things.

Athens, May 1959

Trip

I split your body like sugar cane,
at every knot and every joint
sipping juice from the cracks.
All the while you became more whole
covering me with your rustling leaves,
with the salt-dew of your sea night
and you took me all the way
on a trip from the beast to the human.

                              Sifnos, August 1959

Letter

Our life has become like a letter
bearing some crucial message,
both sender and receiver
lost in the waves of refugees.
The letter comes and goes
from post office to post office
without anyone to open it,
without anyone to throw it away.
The envelope is always marked URGENT
and the names on both sides are fading.
Only postmen read it now,
in the same wise tones used in laboratories
to pronounce the names of extinct species.

                         Paris, November 1959

Cold Wind

And that love for something
you never found or chose
has never left you.
It traversed the noisy days of battle,
it tortured the armed nights,
marked the endless path
you followed—one foot in desire,
the other in resignation.
You couldn't even utter its name.
Still it echoes inside you
like a rush of cold wind in your guts
shaping the frozen shaft
around which your body
stirs, twists, and hopes.

Paris, November 1959

Catacomb

We said: *The sea will always be there*
To grant stones the whiteness of salt.
We said: *There will always be rocks*
To give saltwater the flattened sand.
We were both sure
we resembled stones and sea.
We were sure that whatever happened
some inner motion would toss us together.
Now, nothing drifts between us.
Nothing. We don't admit it openly still.
We just avoid the old similes.
And the difficulty lies not in admitting this new death,
but in setting up another dead man's bust
in those intricate, hidden catacombs of yours.

           Paris, January 1960

Encounter

We met equally and simply.
There was no master or slave.
It all happened with perfect brevity
until we went our separate ways again.
Like a momentary dream of the day
of this encounter
between man and woman.

                          Paris, March 1960

Double Moon

Two eyes rising, a double moon
brightening my life to black and white
behind the fold of dead days.
The more distant these two eyes become
the more they command me.

Paris, May 1960

Metro

And then years will go by,
bulky mountains and stone will intervene,
everything will be forgotten:
just as we forget the daily bread
that sustains us.
Everything, except that moment
when in the crowded Metro
you took hold of my arm.

Paris, May 1960

Via dei Coronari 123

Useless inside the memory, your name
without voices to revive it,
like the lost address of the house
where no one knows I once lived.

                              Rome, September 1961

The Other Town

The day after the dream
a sun came up so black
the blind
saw double darkness.

                        Rome, September 1961

Besieged Time

We thought we knew each other well.
But when our tired garments began falling away
without pretenses or bartered passion
and our bodies remained unprotected,
it was clear how far that road went,
how time was under siege, and us
two ordinary people, almost unreachable.

Paris, March 1962

Via di Tor Millina

I balance like an acrobat on the rope
binding prediction and memory.
The net, your body, the tower.

                        Rome, April 1962

Villa Adriana

In the beginning I remembered your face clearly.
Your flaxen hair, your bright eyes...
It was like a photograph
tacked above the bed of a private.
And as the days went by the paper faded,
the plaster flaked away, all that remained
on the wall was a blank square,
and then the wall crumbled—
gone are the houses we'll never inhabit again.
All that remains is the space
we had arbitrarily defined—
a point of reference
for random things.

                                        Rome, April 1962

The Message

I met you cast away in a giant city
where people pass by and disappear
inside an oceanic yowl.
It was miraculous how new words
burst from my desert mouth.
I put them in a bottle without promises,
absurd, lolling on the asphalt.
I realized there was nothing to presume,
for this was no longer my first youth
and tact had become an unbearable luxury.

Paris, November 1962

Gare du Nord

The crowd, the loudspeakers, the farewells,
your face immobile at the train window,
requests and promises of those next to me—
everything as if plotted by a filmmaker.
And suddenly I recalled Christos, in Athens,
when he told me to see *Brief Encounter*.
The beloved friend, then an enemy, then a stranger,
the old movie, almost never playing now,
you, who begin to turn into memory
even before the train pulls out.

Paris, August 1963

From *Deformities*
(1959–1963)

Επιμονή μιας πόλης

Κανείς βασιλιάς Μάρκος ούτε του Άγιου Μάρκου το λιοντάρι
κανένα χώρισμα απ' το νυχτερινό ψαλμωδίες, μαγεμένες
νυχτερίδες, ξανθές γυναίκες ξένες, σπαθιά σκουριασμένα
τάφρους, φράγμα μ' αίμα, μέσα βαθιά προαιώνια
γιατί μες στον υγρό πηχτό σα λέπι χρόνο
οι πυρκαγιές ξεσπαθώνουν, σηκώνονται ξανά τη νύχτα
αλείφουν τα σπίτια σαν η μέρα σκυλιά και διψασμένα
φωτισμένουν τα μωρά, φωτίζουν μόνιμα σαν πρωτεύει
τη γειτονιά με τα λιπόσαρκα παιδιά τη χιμαιρική πόρνη
με τη γριά που αλησμονεί πότε θα ξημερώσει
να διασούν μ' άλλη μιά φορά τα φυραμένα μέρη τους
τίποτα, κανένας στόχος δεν πρόκειται να 'ρθεί
ούτε κι οι φήμες με προδοσία επιβεβαιώνονται
μένουν τ' ατομεναέρια από μάχες αντιτορπιλικά
στο ψηλό στο μουσείο κι οι ναύτες επιδαψιλευτικά περαστικοί
απ' το παλιό λιμάνι που όσο το ψυχρή κι άγρυος
δεν μπορείς όσο να αιτιάσαι γενική συνθήκες
ηλικίες, δόγματα, ομολογίες πίστεων, στρατηγικές
άλλωστε το πιο αδρανές ατσάλι το δένουμε μονάχοι
δίχως μια τέτοια ιδέα ατομικίτσα να επιβιώσει

Persistence of a City

Neither King Mark nor the lion of Saint Mark,
no distinction between night psalms, incantation,
bats, foreign blondes, rusty swords,
trenches, canyons of blood, continued deep hate,
because inside this pale, lymph-thick time
blazes become vampires, rise again at night
to lick the houses like tame, thirsty dogs,
swaddle babies, light up in luxurious reds
the neighborhoods of skinny children, famished whores,
and old women awaiting daybreak
to bask their sick limbs in sunshine once more.
Nothing, no fleet is going to come,
nor are the rumors of treason verified:
what remains are the ruins of galleys and destroyers
in the closed museum, gaudy seamen strolling
past the old port that silts up with sand.
You can no longer blame the general conditions,
ages, doctrines, confessions of faith, commitments,
even though the most unbreakable steel is made solely by us.
Without such an idea it's impossible to survive;
it gives me the continuity I seek in a perfect sphere.
Otherwise I dissolve into burning dust,
I disperse into passions I don't have time to suspect,
into poisoned gifts I once dreamt of offering.
The ship still follows its extra schedule
into a darkness that devours mountains now.
Your fingers protrude like narrow lines of light,
pointing to the reflection of a city that persists
while nearby some passengers say *La Canea, La Canea.*

From *Optional Stop*
(1967–1973)

Μυστική ζωή

Σοῦ μίλαγα γιά τή μυστική ζωή μου
μά ἴσα τήν ἤξερα ἀπό ξενόγλωσσα βιβλία.
Χρονολογίες, περιστατικά, ἐξηγήσεις—
μπροστά σέ τέτοια βεβαιότητα
τά μυστικά μου γίνονταν ὑποθέσεις ἐργασίας.

Σεπτέμβρης, 1967

Secret Life

I was speaking to you about my secret life,
but you already knew of it from books in foreign tongues.
Dates, events, explanations—
faced with such certainties
my secrets were becoming working hypotheses.

September 1967

Pretense

Everything I asked for was given
and I wasted everything given to me,
or it was reclaimed by the creditors.
Now I think I will dress up in snow
with the pretense of a rational mammoth
that after thousands of years
wants to be found intact.

                                        December 1967

Demonstration

When we joined hands night was already setting in,
crowds were gushing from agitated streets.
In the streets, our life was thrown away;
in the crowd our life is reconstructed.

May 1968

The Mountains

In the beginning was the sea.
I was born among islands,
me too an island that emerged temporarily,
just in time to see light—this also like a stone—
and then sink back again.

The mountains came later.
I chose them.
Somehow I must share the weight
that for ages pressed this country down.

May 1968

Church of the Seven Sleepers

In the moonlight that covered the island
it was as if the sunken volcano opened again,
our hands transformed into octopi
seeking familiar bodies out of reach
till they retreated to their dark chambers.
White fingers, white tentacles, white joints—
in their humid cavity
the palms struggled to hold
the shape of your ever-changing body,
and you too changed, it wasn't you any longer:
you were the seven women I loved
and I was the seven sleeping children
who were martyred, dead seven times.
Each time I reach out to touch you
I find the sea, the stones, the moon,
which all exist beyond us and ignore us.
The same way for years now everyone ignores
the fact that I've been buried in the courtyard
of this deserted, forgotten church.

December 1968

The Stone

Again the same arrogance:
to chisel your life on another life,
as if you wanted to withdraw
your own figure from inside the stone,
believing you had liberated it.

                                        September 1969

Foreign Skies

Always foreign, we turn
from country to country, from city to city.
The little glint of the home country
in the corner of the eye
always fading
under foreign skies.

December 1969

Waiting Area

How can you go on living among people
who died before their time?
How can you continue waiting with the dead
who refuse to believe they ever lived?

January 1970

Woman

I

You brought back my land.
Light and red dirt
stomped upon by tyrants and enemies.
You brought back the storms
of the autumn sea
that rinsed the dust
from my face
and I felt beneath my flesh
the same spine of mountains
that through the years
kept the homeland standing.

II

You brought back my language.
Old words, buried
in ruins and ash,
now come to light,
and the day brightens
as when the world was first made.
Raw metal of words,
thirst, and adequacy
of communication.

III

You brought back the flow of time,
sometimes accelerating, other times
retarding the hours

that now irrigate my barren fields
without covering
any of my statues.

IV

You brought back my city,
which lives and changes away from me,
containing our houses that disappeared
and the river that was covered over.

V

You brought back the dream.
Unknown sea, unexplored
sea of mine,
volcanic island,
a bet with death.
Not knowing if we'll sink again
or if we'll surface even higher.

October 1970

The Journey

Death demands his drachma
no matter what threshold you cross,
no matter what journey.
Not everyone is able to pay;
not everyone travels first class.

                                      January 1971

Oedipus's Story

He wanted to solve the riddles,
cast light on the darkness
everyone feels at ease with,
no matter how heavy it is upon them.
What scared him most wasn't what he saw,
but the refusal of the others to see it.
Would he always be the exception?
He couldn't stand loneliness anymore.
In order to find his neighbors
he thrust the two pins
deep into his eyes.
He still understood by touch
things nobody wanted to see.

January 1971

Easter

They greeted the arrival of love with palms.
Then they crucified it themselves,
pierced it with a spear,
watered it with vinegar and bile,
put it out with the thieves.
Still, they awaited resurrection for their sake.

January 1971

Millennia

Each second and a drop,
each drip and a molecule of salt.
The stalagmites have risen,
the stalactites have fallen.
Perhaps the miracle
of our meeting will occur
in the millennia to come.

January 1971

Allegory

When the oak tree fell
some people cut a branch, slammed it in the soil,
calling the others to worship the same tree;
some others lamented with elegies
the lost forest, their lost lives;
others made collections of dried leaves,
exhibited them in fairs, earned a living;
others affirmed the destructiveness of deciduous trees,
disagreeing, though, about how to, or even whether to
    reforest;
others, and me with them, maintained that as long as
there are earth and seeds, there exists the possibility
of an oak tree.

The problem of water remains open.

June 1973

From *Opposing Mirrors*
(1988)

Πόλη της νότιας Ελλάδας

Ετούτη η πόλη με σακατεύει, όπως παλιά
μπορούσε μια πόλη να με σακατεύει,
με τους στρατώνες της τ' άδεια εργοστάσια
τους μαύρους τοίχους με τα κοφτερά γυαλιά
με τους στενούς της δρόμους, άδυτη, στυγνή
με τις υφάλμυρες μελαγχολικές γυναίκες της
εύκαμπτες, ρευστές, κάρβουνα μάτια
δέρματα λαδιά, μια στάλα ιδρωμένη
όσο χρειάζεται για έρωτα περαστικό και φευγαλέο
σ' αφώτιστη μισότερμες ακροδαλασσιές
με πέτσες, πίσσες, σκουριές, αμμάδια.
Ετούτη η πόλη με ματώνει με τη νύχτη της
νύχτη του τόπου μου που δεν αλλάζουν.

Verses, 3

No verse overthrows regimes
I wrote one day many years ago,
and up till now I've been charged with it.
But verses do their job—
they point at the regime, they call them out,
even when the regimes try to fancify themselves,
to renovate the window displays a little,
change their brand name and label.
Surely verses catch the leaders by surprise
in unexpected positions,
in their yellowed and unbuttoned underwear
when they are certain nobody is watching;
and before they put on their breeches or trousers,
with bony legs and bedraggled slippers;
before they pull on their boots or wingtips,
with their guts overspilling till they suck them in
so they can button up their marching coats or blazers;
their dentures left in a cup
before they rehearse again their history-making sermons;
with their double chins and sagging cheeks
before they proudly lift those chins;
before they peer into the future, remaining always young.
Verses do not overthrow regimes,
but certainly they outlive all the regime's placards.

                              30 November 1982

A Town in Southern Greece

This town has crippled me, the same way
a town could cripple me in the past,
with its barracks, its empty factories—
the black walls topped with broken glass,
with its narrow streets, treeless, dry,
with its dark, salty women,
agile and fluid, with coal black eyes,
olive-skinned, sweaty enough
for a quick, fleeting love
along dim, half-deserted sea sides,
with their stones, tar, rust, and thorns.
This town heals me with its nights,
nights of my country that do not change.

Zebras

Light through adjustable wooden *persiennes*
of half-closed hotel shutters,
to the left of the train station's square,
light cast in shreds
dressing us up in zebra skin:
two zebras wrestling in light and darkness,
black and white stripes drawn
diagonally by the headlights of cars,
black and white immersion in your body.
So many years later, I sometimes see again
black and white zebra flutings on my skin
each time I stay alone in a seaside town hotel.

From *The Pleasures of Extension*
(1992)

My Language

My language wasn't easy to
    keep safe
among the languages that were trying
    to devour it
yet in my language I persisted in
    counting,
in my language I brought time down
    to the measure of the body,
in my language I multiplied
    pleasure to the infinite,
and with that I brought back the memory
    of a child
with a white scar from a stone strike
    on his shaved head.
I struggled not to lose
    a single word of it
since in that language
    even the dead spoke to me.

Loves

A love is born within love,
grows up within its guts
expands in its space, inhabits it,
desires duration, struggles for time,
prevails, enjoys its supremacy,
and once it relaxes in conquest
another love is born in its guts,
grows up, expands in its space,
threatens to eat it up.
But loves finally cease
feeding on antagonistic flesh;
they just exchange stone facsimiles
that remain untouched in their decay,
coexist without pointless hostility,
almost amicable, like the busts
of rival political leaders in graveyards.

Appropriation of Statues

We make statues out of the matter
from statues made by other craftsmen
who came before;
we make poems with words
from poems written
in the past, by other poets;
we make lives out of emotions and talents
other people before us
had experienced.
We appropriate works, modify
plans, change perspectives,
invent something new;
we make things entirely ours,
always leaving behind traces
of a prior origin.
We continue by putting our names
next to other names,
even next to those
we would like to erase.

From *Resistance of the Facts*
(2000)

Η τέφρα

Δεν ήσαν οι ζωντανοί που μ' εμποδίζανε
μαζί τους τα κατάφερνα
όσο κι αν με φορτώνανε με χρέη.
Εκείνοι που με δέσμευαν ήσαν οι νεκροί
τους έθαβα μια δεύτερη φορά, μια τρίτη
πάλι με δέχονταν δικό τους.
Ακόμα κι όταν καίγονταν δεν γλίτωνα
η τέφρα τους ξαναρχόταν με τον άνεμο
έπεφτε και κολλούσε πάνω μου.
Μόνο άμα βολεύθηκα ν' αλλάξω
τη μνήμη τους σε λόγια
που πετούσαν σαν πουλιά
ένιωσα σιγά σιγά να λευτερώνομαι.

Ashes

It was not the living that held me back—
I dealt with them
in spite of the debts they heaved on me.
It was the dead who held me in chains.
I kept burying them: two times, a third,
but they still wanted me for themselves.
Even after they were burnt I couldn't escape,
their ashes kept riding back down the wind
falling and clinging to me.
Only when I put down their memory
in words that flew like birds,
then little by little I freed myself.

Nightmare

If the dead see that dream
then their nightmare must be
to come back to life.

Molyvos, 1

—for Yiannis and
Rallou Constandellis

The same landscape for ages:
the stone houses,
the castle, the cobbled streets,
the olive trees, the beach.
The same landscape,
with a few changes
that would be noted by Alcaeus, Sappho,
Arion, Longus.
The same landscape where
I myself arrived
in the boats of the Athenians
from the other bank.
Opposite: Troy,
Assos, Asia,
the world, as I see it,
wide, terrific, beautiful.

Molyvos, 2

I look from my window
at the pomegranate tree.
In the distance, a sea
more cerulean than ever,
and green leaves deeper
engraved in the blue,
today the pomegranates
redder than yesterday.
I see how much the tree
I planted ten years ago
has grown. I look at
the pomegranates, which
flourished this year.
I look at the sea in the distance
and I return to my writing.

The Young Researcher

The young researcher was studying
once again from the beginning those reasons
why a dedication to faith
brought death to some
and material benefit to others;
why worship turned into hate,
admiration into scorn;
why final decisions were overturned
even by the judges themselves.

At last he began to discern the mechanisms
that turned ideas
into a mere rhetoric of ideas;
friendly meetings
into patrolled reunions;
lovers' embraces
into workouts at the gym;
he could discern in photos of the new age
the spots of old age.
But he couldn't perceive
the sentiments of those who
sacrificed themselves freely,
or those who tried in vain
to avoid it,
even those whose task was
to sacrifice and file people away.

Everything was part of the game
in a century still in its death-agony,
or rather it was the resistance of the facts,
the researcher thought, as he typed
on the keyboard of his computer.

Violence

I try to call things
by their names,
but every now and then I encounter
new difficulties.
For example, to call violence *violence*,
not *peacemaking intervention*—
the violence of the rich and powerful—
nor *inevitable extremity*—
the violence of the poor and oppressed.
I find difficulty in the alterations
of what we call historical necessity,
reversals in the movements of politicians,
innumerable analyses by their spokesmen;
but mainly I feel perplexed
by my own interpretations and guilt.
I would like to say openly at last
that I've come to detest,
whoever it belongs to, all violence.

The Final Evening of a Poetry Festival

Before a large audience
I'm reading poems
from various decades
and they all seem to me
as if written just now.
It's hard to remember
with any precision
everything that happened
when each was being set down.
All those important events
that riled the world
are almost forgotten now,
as I have almost forgotten
loves, travails, journeys
that at the time
I considered unique.

I'm reading poems
written at times
when mostly I listened.
There are fewer new ones now
that I am mostly listened to.
Still, there are always
moments unique in their way,
ony they are forgotten quicker,
like lines not written in time.

I'm reading poems from various decades,
deleting their dates
so nothing stalls the movement of the years.

From *The Lions' Gate*
(2002)

Τεχνάσματα τοῦ Ὀδυσσέα

Στὸν Δημήτρη Μαρωνίτη

Ὁ Ὀδυσσέας ἤξερε γιὰ τὸ σόφισμα
πολὺ πρὶν ἀπ' τὸν Σηνωνα
ἤξερε πὼς ὁ χρόνος δὲν τεμαχίζεται
πὼς ὁ Ἀχιλλέας ξεπερνάει στὸ τρέξιμο τὴ χελώνα
γιὰ νὰ τὸν παραπλανήσει, πολυμήχανος ὅπως ἦταν
ἔβαλε στὴ γραμμὴ ἀναρίθμητη χελῶνες
ἔτσι κάποια βρισκόταν πάντοτε μπροστὰ
ἀπὸ τὸν γοργοπόδαρο ἥρωα.
Ὁ Ὀδυσσέας ἔμαθε μὲ τὸν πόλεμο
πὼς οὔτε νὰ ἀναστρέφεται ὁ χρόνος
ὅπως μετὰ τὸν γυρισμὸ πάλι δοκίμασε
μερικὰ τεχνάσματα μήπως γίνει ὅπως πρὶν
ἀκατανίκητος ἐραστὴς κι ἐρωτυμένος σύζυγος
γοῦ μαγάπητος βασιλιὰς γιὰ μοναχινὸς ταξιδευτὴς
ὥστου τὸ παραδέχτηκε δημόσια
ὁ χρόνος μπορεῖ νὰ σωρεύει χρῆμα
ν' ἀνάγει περιπέτειη, νὰ συρρικνώνει τὸ ἄγνωστο
μὰ τίποτα ἀπ' ὅλα αὐτὰ δὲν φέρνει πίσω
τὸν περασμένο χρόνο ποὺ τὰ γέννησε.
Ὁ Ὀδυσσέας ἔνιωσε ὅτι γερνούσε

The Wiles of Odysseus
—for Dimitris Maronitis

Odysseus knew about casuistry
long before Zeno;
he knew that time cannot be clipped;
that Achilles beats a turtle in a footrace,
but to trick him, being so resourceful,
he set up numerous turtles
so there was always one
ahead of that swift hero.
Odysseus also learned from war
that time cannot be reversed.
But after coming home, he employed
his wiles again, hoping to become as he was
    before:
an irresistible lover and a husband in love,
a popular king and lonesome traveler,
until he admitted in public
that time may indeed accumulate money,
open up adventures, shrink the unknown,
but none of the above could give back
the past that created them.
Odysseus felt, growing old,
that whatever he saw and suffered
was enough for others but not for him.
In spite of tonics and herbs for longevity,
it became more difficult to invent
new things to fill up
his always-expanding desires.

Of Pikes and Warriors

—for Lucio Mariani

A poet friend from Italy was talking to me
about the *sarissa* of Alexander the Great,
who dashes in battle to lance Darius
as depicted in the mosaic of Pompeii:
the multitude of inclined or horizontal spears
that bring death along with beauty;
they resembled, he continued, the moving pikes
in the painted triptych of battles by Uccello.
Or the erect pikes by Velasquez,
I added, in the *Surrender of Breda,*
even the golden pikes
by Rembrandt, in *The Night Watch.*
So lovely, those dense pikes, forests
of thin trunks, hewn branches sturdy
with their shiny iron tips:
you forget death, only beauty remains.
Only at night I considered
how the body must suffer when the lance
is thrust down to its dark bowels,
how it groans, convulses until it expires.
But in my memory again emerged the beauty
of colorful depictions, of countless pikes,
and thousands of warriors on stage
fearless against the onslaught of time.

Notes

"Earth and Sea"
Patrikios was twenty-six years old when this poem was first published in 1954. The pastoral environment described in this poem is the island of Ai-Stratis (see note below).

"Drafts on Makronissos"
Makronissos is a barren island off the coast of Attica, near Kea. It was used to imprison members of the leftist parties that were outlawed by the British and American-backed government, led by Prime Minister Sofoulis, in 1946. There, prisoners were subjected to torture, hard labor, and solitary confinement. In addition to Patrikios, the poet Yiannis Ritsos and the composer Mikis Theodorakis were detained there. It was repopulated with inmates again by the military junta that ruled Greece from 1967–73.

"BETO, AETO, CETO, SFA, the Gamma Center": these are the names of the various detention centers, listed as they were located north to south. Skarvellas was the prison guard assigned to keep watch over Patrikios.

The phrase "Embros ELAS yia teen Ellada" is from a partisan anthem; ELAS is the acronym for the leftist Popular Greek Liberation Army, famous for its resistance activities against German occupation, but later outlawed.

"Another Day on Ai-Stratis"
Like Makronissos, the island of Agios Efstratios (or Ai-Stratis) was used as a detainment camp. It is located in the northern Aegean, off the coast of Lemnos and is, unlike Makronissos, both beautiful and inhabited (by a small population of fishermen, farmers, and their families).

"Military March"
Detainees were forced to sing propagandistic songs and military marches while laboring on Makronissos.

"Monologue"
The imagery of this poem is informed by the fact that Patrikios suffered from tuberculosis during his imprisonment. This fact was not lost on his guards, who frequently placed him in solitary confinement in a ravine without blankets or kerosene heaters.

"Night in the Tent"
The unpublished poet Costas Koulafakos was a close friend of Patrikios in detention.

"Elements of Identity"
This poem sparked a small controversy in the 1960s since it was thought by certain members of the left to typify a poetry of the movement's defeat. Nikita Kruschev's "Special Report to the Twentieth Congress of the Communist Party of the Soviet Union" was famous for its denunciation of Stalin, a condemnation in particular of the "cult of the individual" and the subsequent failures Stalin had inspired. Here, Patrikios looks forward ironically to what might be achieved in a fictional "Thirtieth Congress."

"Persistence of a City"
"La Canea" is the Italian name for Chania, a city on Crete colonized by the Venetians from the fourteenth through the sixteenth centuries.

"Molyvos, 1"
Ancient Methymna, on the northern coast of the island of Lesbos facing the Turkish towns of Troy and Assos, is now known as Molyvos. Alcaeus and Sappho, both lyric poets, were contemporaries on Lesbos in sixth century BCE. Arion of Lesbos is credited with inventing the dithyramb. Longus, who may have lived on Lesbos, gave us the pastoral novel *Daphnis and Chloe,* which is set there.

"Church of the Seven Sleepers"
According to legend, persecuted by the Roman emperor Decius, seven young Christian men fled to a cave where they slept—for a miraculously long time—and awoke to find themselves in a newly Christian empire. A famous shrine to the Seven Sleepers has been excavated on Mount Pion, outside Ephesus.

"Of Pikes and Warriors"
The innovation of the *sarissa*—enormous, double-spiked pikes—gave the Macedonian phalanx, led by Alexander, an intimidating advantage in countless battles.

About Titos Patrikios

Titos Patrikios was born in Athens in 1928. He was active in the resistance movement against the German Occupation, but during the years of military dictatorship following the Greek Civil War he was "displaced" within the borders of his own country (to detention camps on the islands of Makronissos and Ai-Stratis), and later exiled outright to Paris and Rome. After he received Greece's National Prize for Literature, Patrikios's numerous books were assembled by Kedros Publishers into a three-volume *Collected Poems;* several new volumes have followed. This is the first full-length collection of his poems in English.

About the Translators

Christopher Bakken is the author of two books of poems: *Goat Funeral* (Sheep Meadow Press, 2006) and *After Greece* (Truman State University Press), which won the 2001 T. S. Eliot Prize for Poetry. His poems, essays, and translations have appeared widely. He teaches at Allegheny College in Meadville, Pennsylvania.

Roula Konsolaki received degrees from Aristotle University of Thessaloniki and Kapodistrian University of Athens. Now living in Crete, she teaches at a state school and works as a freelance translator from French and English into Greek. Her translations have been printed or are forthcoming in *Modern Poetry in Translation, Two Lines, Seneca Review, Literary Imagination, The Tampa Review,* and elsewhere. She is also the translator of *Kai Meta tin Ellada Ti...* (published in the U.S. as *After Greece*), by Christopher Bakken.

Τα λιοντάρια ήχων
ούτε ένα δεν βρίσκ...
ή μάλλον ένα μονα-
χόν ήχε ... φτι
χμέν ... στη ... π...
ω τ... το σπίτων κ
σ... ή δύπησα
ποτέ δεν έπαψ...
τε ...μαψε ή εικόνα